نشوان

شهد شريف محمد ياسين

اسم الكتاب : نشروان

تأليف : شهد شريف محمد ياسين

تصميم الغلاف : سها عبدالنبي

الإخراج الفني : فريق عمل بصمة كاتب

تنسيق : سارة عيد

تصنيف الكتاب : خواطر

المقاس : ١٤ × ٢٠

إصدار : ٢٠٢٤

رقم الإيداع : ٢٠٢٤/٨٢٨٤

مديرة الدار : حبيبة شبل

للتواصل والاستفسار / 01093187904

نشروان

إن الحمد لله نحمده ونستعينه ونستغفره ونستهديه ونعوذ بالله تعالى من شرور أنفسنا ومن سيئات أعمالنا من يهده الله فلا مضل له، ومن يضلل فلا هادي له وأشهد أن لا أله إلا الله وأن محمد عبده ورسوله أما بعد: فهذا الكتيب تحدثت فيه عن موضوعات شتى، لعل كلماتي البسيطة تدخل قلب أحد وتكون سبب في هدايته، ما كان من توفيق فمن الله وماكان من خطأ أو سهو فمني ومن الشيطان اللهم اغفر لنا ذنوبنا وإسرافنا في أمرنا وثبت أقدامنا وانصرنا على القوم الكافرين

الله

رأيت الله في كل شيء لم يتركني رغم ما أفعله من معاصي كان وما زال رحيما بي يعطيني ما أتمناه إن كان خيرا لي ويصرفه عني إن كان شرا لي، فالله هو الركن الشديد الذي نركن إليه جميعا، ونستريح من ضجيج هذه الحياة المتعثرة، أعطانا الكثير ولكننا لا نرض بما قسمه لنا، وقد ذكر الله ذلك في القرآن العظيم قال تعالى "وإن تعدوا نعمة الله لا تحصوها إن الإنسان لظلوم كفار" وقال أيضا "وإن تعدوا نعمة الله لا تحصوها إن الله لغفور رحيم" في هذه الآيات ذكر الله لنا معاملة العباد له عز وجل ومعاملته تعالى لنا الله رغم كل ما نفعله مازال رحيما بنا، فأحوالنا ستسري على أي حال ولكن بما قسمه الله لك وسترى جبره العظيم لقلبك

لك أرفع الشكوى بغير تكلم

يا ذا الجلال الواهب المتكرم

الحال لا يشكي لغيرك سيدي

يا كاشف البلوى عن المتألم

إن لم تكن أنت الملاذ لغربتي

فبمن ألوذ وأستجير وأحتمي

God

I saw God in everything. He did not abandon me, despite the sins I committeed. He was and still is merciful to me. He gives me what I wish for If it is good for me, and turns it away from me if it is bad for me. God is the strong pillar upon which we all rely, and we find relief from the noise of this troubled life. He has given us much, but we We are not satisfied with what He has apportioned for us, and God mentioned that In the Great Qur'an. The Almighty said, "And if you exceed the blessing of God, you cannot count it. Indeed, mankind is unjust and disbelievers." He also said, "And if you exceed the blessing of God, you cannot count it. Indeed, God is Forgiving, Merciful." In these verses, God mentioned to us how His servants treat Him. God Almighty and His treatment of us, God Almighty, despite everything we do, is still merciful to us, our conditions will apply anyway, but be satisfied with what God has divided for you and you will see His great redress for your heart

I file the complaint without speaking

O Majesty, the Most Generous Giver

The situation does not complain to anyone but you, sir

O Revealer of calamity from the suffering

If you are not the refuge for my alienation

To whom can I seek refuge, seek refuge, and seek refuge

العائلة

بدونكم لا يكن للنجاح لذة، ولا نشعر بحلاوة هذه الحياة، أنتم الأنس والسكينة لنا بدونكم نحن لاشيء، كل حزن يهون وأنتم جواري مهما تكلمنا لا نوفي حقكم علينا، لولاكم ما شفيت تلك الجروح ولا التئمت، العائلة هي الأمان والطمأنينة لكل إنسان، نحن مدينون بكل الحب لكم وأسمى عبارات الشكر، ما أجمل ابتسامتنا معكم!

The Family

Without you, success has no pleasure, and we do not feel the sweetness of this life. You are comfort and tranquility for us. Without you, we are nothing. Every sadness is lessened while you are by our side. No matter how much we talk, we do not fulfill your right to us. Without you, these wounds would not have healed or healed. The family is safety and reassurance for every human being. We owe everything... Love to you and the highest expressions of thanks, how beautiful our smile is with you!

أمي

أمي عجزت الحروف عن وصفكِ، فا أنت أعظم من أن تحتويكِ كلماتي، عندما أتحدث عنكِ فإنني أتحدث عن أعظم انتصاراتي في هذه الحياة، فبدونك لا معنى لحياتي، فوجودك يُسكر قلبي المتعب، عندما أنظر إلى القمر أتذكر وجهك البشوش الذي كاد أن يسابق القمر في الجمال، كثيرا ما أتعبك، ولكن أحبك كثيرا، وأحاول دوما أن أسعدك فقد قال ربي "ووصينا الإنسان بوالديه إحسانا حملته أمه كرها ووضعته كرها" فا بركِ غايتي أنت الشخص الذي لن يتكرر في حياتي مرة أخرى سأظل أحافظ عليكِ يا أمي.

My mom

My mother, words cannot describe you. You are too great for my words to contain you. When I talk about you, I am talking about my greatest victories in this life. Without you, my life has no meaning. Your presence intoxicates my tired heart. When I look at the moon, I remember your smiling face that almost rivaled the moon in beauty. I often tire you, but I love you very much, and I always try to make you happy. My Lord said, "And We have enjoined upon man to be kind to his parents. His mother carried him hard and gave birth to him hard." So, bless you, my goal. You are the person who will never happen again in my life. I will always protect you, my mother.

الأب

تُرى ماهو الأب؟

أرى كل الآباء كنجمة ساطعة تضيء حياة أبنائهم، فإذا اختفت هذه النجمة أصبحت حياتهم معتمة، لابد من وجود الآباء؛ لكي تصبح حياتنا أكثر استقرارا، فهم السند والأمان لنا،قد نرى عصبيته الشديدة علينا في بعض الأوقات، ولكن هذا من حبه لنا وحرصه علينا، عندما نطلب شيئا يلبيه، وإن لم يستطع يبذل قصارى جهده؛ لكي يأتي بما نريد، أهذا الشخص لا يستحق أن نُسعد قلبه؟

بلى يستحق أكثر من هذا يستحق أن نجتهد في دراستنا، ولا نضيع أوقاتنا في الهراء، وأن ننجح بمعدل عال؛ كي يفرح قلب ذاك الشخص الذي تعب كثيرا؛ ليوفر لنا النقود والملبس والمأكل رغما عنه، مهما كبرنا لا نستطع أن نوفيه حقه، فا أنت يا أبي لم تكن شخصا عاديا في يوم، أنت الهواء الذي أتنفسه ولا أستطع أن أعيش بدونه.

ما أعظم الآباء!

ما أجمل وجودهم الدافئ في حياتنا!

The father

What is the father?

I see all fathers as a bright star that illuminates their children's lives. If this star disappears, their lives become dark. Fathers must exist; In order for our lives to become more stable, they are our support and security. We may see his extreme nervousness toward us at times, but this Is from his love for us and his concern for us. When we ask for something, he grants it, and if he is not able to do his best; In order to get what we want, does this person not deserve to make his heart happy?

Indeed, he deserves more than this. He deserves that we work hard in our studies, not waste our time on nonsense, and that we succeed at a high rate, To rejoice the heart of that person who is very tired; To provide us with money, clothing, and food against his will. No matter how old he grows, we cannot fulfill his rights. You, my father, were not an ordinary person one day. You are the air that I breathe and I cannot live without you.

What great fathers!

How beautiful is their warm presence in our lives!

المعلم

من كالمعلم؟ يبذل قصارى جهده من أجل طلابه، يعاملنا كأبنائه ويجود علينا بعطاءاته الكثيرة، فالمعلم كثيرا ما يكون بمثابة أب لنا بنصائحه وخوفه علينا من الضياع، ويعمل دوما على أن نتقدم إلى الأمام، أتذكر أنني كنت أعاني من مادة الرياضيات، وأراها من أصعب المواد التي مرت عليّ لكن عندما أخذت درسا بدأ معلمي يحدثني عنها كعلم وبدأت أستسهلها، فا هذا المعلم جعلني أحب مادة الرياضيات التي كانت تشكل لي كارثة كبيرة، فا أنا لن أنسى فضله، فعلينا جميعا أن نعي أهمية العلماء، وأن قيمتهم تكون مرفوعة عند الله تعالى حيث قال عز وجل "إنما يخشى الله من عباده العلماؤوا" وهم أيضا ورثة الأنبياء، فا أي شرف هذا وأي مكانة هذه

لولا المعلم ما كان الأطباء

ولا تفنن في الإعمار بناء

فلتكرموه ولا تقسوا عليه فما

أهانه غير من في عقله داء

داء الجهالة بالإذلال يدفننا

والعلم نور به للمجد إحياء

معلمي سوف تبقى لي السراج

وإن بعدت عني فللأرواح إسراء.

حقا إنها مهنة عظيمة.الجمال.

The teacher

Who is like a teacher? He does his best for his students. He treats us like his children and gives us his many gifts. The teacher is often like a father to us with his advice and his fear for us of loss, and he alwayss works to make us move forward. I remember that I was suffering from mathematics, and I see it as one of the most difficult subjects that I have ever experienced. But when I took a lesson, my teacher started telling me about it as a science and I started to find it easy. This teacher made me love mathematics, which was a huge disaster for me. I will never forget his virtue. We must all be aware of the importance of scientists, and that their value Is elevated to God Almighty, as the Almighty said: "Only among His servants are scholars who fear God." They are also heirs of the prophets, so what honor is this and what status is this?Without the teacher, there would be no doctors

And do not be creative In constructive reconstruction

Honor him and do not be harsh on him

He insulted someone other than someone who has a disease in his mind

The disease of ignorance with humiliation buries us

Knowledge is a light that brings glory to life

My teacher will keep me going

And if you are far from me, then the souls have Isra.

It really Is a great profession.Beauty.

الصداقة

قارئي الأصدقاء بمثابة روح أخرى لنا، معهم يحلوا أوقاتنا ونشعر بمتعة الحياة، فهم الملاذ والأمان لأرواحنا، فالأصدقاء أعظم ما أنجبته لنا الأيام نكون معهم أكثر فرحا وأكثر إقبالا على الحياة، فنحن بدون أصدقائنا نشعر بالوحدة ووحشة الدنيا، محظوظ من يمتلك صديق مخلصا له ويحبه بصدق، فأصبح الآن لا يحب بعضنا بعض إلا القليل الصادق، فالصديق الوفي يأخذ مكانة كبيرة في القلب ويكون كالأخ نشاركه في أدق تفاصيلنا، أعظم صداقة لن تتكرر في التاريخ هي صداقة سيدنا محمد صلى الله عليه وسلم وسيدنا أبو بكر رضي الله عنه وأرضاه.

ما أحلى الأصدقاء!

The friendship

Friends who read are like another soul to us. With them they brighten our time and we feel the joy of life. They are the refuge and security for our souls. Friends are the greatest thing that the days have given us. We are with them more joy and more interested in life. Without our friends, we feel lonely and lonely in the world. Lucky is the one who has a friend who is loyal to him and loves him sincerely. Now we do not love each other except the sincere few. The loyal friend occupies a great place in the heart and Is like a brother with whom we share our smallest details. The greatest friendship that will not be repeated in history is the friendship of our master Muhammad, may God bless him and grant him peace, and our master Abu Bakr, may God be pleased with him and please him.

What sweet friends!

الحب

منذ الوهلة الأولى وسهم حبك أصابني، لم تمر علي عيونك مرار الكرام فعندما أنظر إليهما أشعر بالطمأنينة أتعجب أهذه عيناك أم ملجأ لي من ضجيج الحياة؟

أنا الآن غارقة في حبك وأنت وحدك من يستطع إنقاذي، أحبك من صميم قلبي، فا أصبحت أنت القلب والحياة، أحب جلوسنا معا وتناولنا القهوة أحب نظرات عيونك المليئة بالحب لي، أصبحت تداويني عندما أتألم،أفتقد لحظاتي من دونك، يا حبيبي لا تغب طويلا عن هذا القلب فإنه يعاني كثيرا من دونك، حظيت بك بعد كل هذا العناء فا لن أفلت يدي من يديك، ليتكم تذوقوا حلاوة الحب فإنه أعظم شعور عرفته البشرية،الروح إن قابلت من تحب ترممت وتعافت، ما أدفئ لحظاتنا مع من نحب!

Love

From the first moment, the arrow of your love struck me. Your eyes have never been unnoticed by me. When I look at them, I feel reassured. I wonder, are these your eyes or a refuge for me from the noise of life?

I am now immersed in your love and you are the only one who can save me. I love you from the bottom of my heart, so you have become my heart and life. I love us sitting together and having coffee. I love the looks in your eyes full of love for me. You heal me when I am in pain. I miss my moments without you, my love, do not be away from this for long. The heart suffers a lot without you. I had you after all this trouble, so I will not let go of your hands. I wish you could taste the sweetness of love, for it is the greatest feeling known to humanity. If the soul meets the one it loves, it is repaired and recovered. How warm our moments are with the one we love!

أينسى أحد قلبه؟

كان السواد يملأ حياتي حتى أتيت إليها وملأتها بالنور الذي يشع من عينيك، أتساءل دائمًا عن أي فعل جزاني الله إياك؟

فا أنت العوض لي بعد كل هذه السنين المؤلمة، عندما أرى ابتسامتك تُمحى كل أحزاني، وكأن الحب يجعلنا أكثر سعادة وأكثر إقبالا على هذه الحياة بوجود الحبيب ما أعظم الأشياء التي تكون بطعم الحب!

Does anyone forget his heart?

Blackness filled my life until you came to it and filled it with the light that shines from your eyes. I always wonder for what action God rewarded you for?

You are my compensation after all these painful years. When I see your smile, all my sorrows are erased. It is as if love makes us happier and more willing to live this life with the presence of the beloved. How great are the things that taste like love!

يا للهول! أهذه ابتسامتُكَ أم سحر لقلبي؟

كم أحبك أكثر من نفسي أنتَ لا تعلم مقدار عشقي لك عندما دخلت حياتي جاءت معك السعادة لقلبي المتعب، واطمأنت نفسي، وأشرقت ابتسامتي من جديد أراك نجمي الوحيد الذي بدونه يحل الظلام على حياتي.

أيا نجم في سمائي هل ما زلت لا تعلم مقدار حبي لك؟

Oh my God! Is this your smile or magic for my heart?

How much I love you more than myself. You do not know how much I love you. When you entered my life, you brought happiness to my tired heart, reassured myself, and made my smile shine again. I see you are my only star, without which darkness falls on my life.

Oh star in my sky, do you still not know how much I love you?

الفقد

الواحدة ظهرا تلقيت اتصالا أن صديقي مات لم تصدق أذني ما سمعت، وقلت أنها مزحة من أصدقائي لكن عندما ذهبت إلى بيته رأيت أنه قد فارق الحياة امتقع وجهي وغثيت، قلبي منذ ذلك اليوم لم يعد كما كان سكنه الحزن والألم كان هذا الصديق أخا لي أصبحت الآن وحيدا رغم كل من حولي لكن هذا الحبيب الذي كنا نتشاكل معا ونضحك معا، الفقد إنه الشعور الأصعب على الإطلاق، لو كان الفقد شخصا لقتلته، ويحدث في فلسطين أن شخصا فقد زوجته وابنيه وحفيده وابنته أيحدث هذا؟

بالطبع حدث ولكنه مازال صامدا، وشخص آخر يُترك أكثر من خمس ساعات يُنزف دمه دون أن ينقذه أحد بالإجبار، ثم تتلقى عائلته خبر وفاته" عزاؤنا أن الملتقى الجنة"، لم أر شيئا يقهر الإنسان مثله تراه يفرق بين الصديقين والحبيبين والأقارب فا الفقد يجعل الشخص هشا ويؤثر علينا بشكل كبير، آهٍ على فقد الأحباب والصحاب.

ما أصعب الفقد على النفس!

Loss

At one o'clock in the afternoon, I received a call that my friend had died. My ears could not believe what I heard. I said it was a joke from my friends, but when I went to his house, I saw that he had passed away. My face became swollen and I felt sick. Since that day, my heart was no longer as it was, filled with sadness and pain. This friend was a brother to me. She has become now. Alone, despite everyone around me, but this beloved, with whom we used to quarrel together and laugh together. Loss is the hardest feeling ever. If loss were a person, I would kill him. It happens in Palestine that a person loses his wife, two sons, his grandson, and his daughter. Does this happen?Of course it happened, but he is still standing, and another person is left bleeding for more than five hours without anyone forcibly saving him. Then his family receives the news of his death. "Our consolation is that the meeting place Is Paradise." I have never seen anything that defeats a person like it. You see it separating friends, lovers, and relatives. Loss makes a person fragile. It affects us greatly, as we mourn the loss of loved ones and friends.

How difficult it Is to hate oneself!

المرأة

هل دور المرأة مقتصرا على الطبخ؟

بلى يوجد للمرأة أدوارا كثيرة، فمنها دورها الكبير والعظيم في الإسلام، دورها كأم وزوجة وأخت، دورها في صنع بيت سعيد، دورها المهم في إصلاح أبنائها نعم المرأة هي التي تصلح أبنائها هذا لا ينفي أن الرجل له دور في إصلاحهم لكن هي التي عليها الجزء الأكبر، هي التي تحمل وتُرضع وتربي لكن ليس الكل يستطيع أن يربي بشكل جيد، سأعطيكم نبذة مختصرة، فقد نرى أم تعطي أبناؤها كل ما يطلبونه في أي وقت شاؤوا لكن إذا قالت لا في مرة ترى أبناؤها يتضجرون ولا يرضون بهذا؛ لأنهم من البداية يأخذون كل ما يرغبون، وأم أخرى تعطي مرة وتمنع مرة، وهذا يكوّن أبناء صالحين، فالمربي يجب أن يكون صارما وحكيما ألا يكون عصبيا على أبنائه؛ كي لا يكبروا مشوهين نفسيا، أن يكون حنونا وعطوفا عليهم فهم ينتظرون هذا منا وتذكري أيها المربية أن أبناءك أمانة من الله عز وجل فا أحسني تربيتهم وحافظي عليهم.

Woman

Is the role of women limited to cooking?

Indeed, women have many roles, including their great and great role in Islam, their role as a mother, wife and sister, their role In creating a happy home, their important role in reforming their children. Yes, it is the woman who reforms her children. This does not deny that the man has a role in reforming them, but she is the one who has the largest role. She is the one who carries, breastfeeds, and raises, but not everyone can raise well. I will give you a brief overview. We may see a mother giving her children everything they ask for at any time they want, but if she says no one time, you will see her children getting bored and not satisfied with this; Because from the beginning they take everything they want,Another mother gives sometimes and withholds sometimes, and this results in good children. The educator must be strict and wise and not be angry with his children. So that they do not grow up psychologically distorted, to be affectionate and compassionate toward them, as they expect this from us. And remember, O nanny, that your children are a trust from God Almighty, so raise them well and take care of them.

الحجاب

أيها القارئ أصبح في زماننا هذا لا تستطع أن تفرق بين البنت المسلمة و المسيحية!!!

تخيل معي إلى أين وصلنا هذا والله ليبكي القلب قبل العين أيا مسلمة تضيعي حجابك لدنيا فانية؟ أمرنا الله تعالى بالحجاب ليحفظنا من آفات لسان الآخرين ليحمينا من مريضين القلب لأننا لسنا كأي شخص نحن فتيات المسلمين لا يستطيع أي شخص أن يصل إلينا بهذه السهولة لذا وضع الله لنا ضوابط للحجاب والاختلاط، فيجب علينا أن نرتدي الحجاب كما أمر الله تعالى: أن يكون ساترا لجميع البدن، وألا يصف، وأن يكون فضفاضا، فا أين أنتِ منه؟ لا تستمعي لمن يقول أن الحجاب يجعلكِ أكبر سنا أنتِ بالحجاب ملكة. قال تعالى"يَا أَيُّهَا النَّبِيُّ قُل لِّأَزْوَاجِكَ وَبَنَاتِكَ وَنِسَاءِ الْمُؤْمِنِينَ يُدْنِينَ عَلَيْهِنَّ مِن جَلَابِيبِهِنَّ ذَٰلِكَ أَدْنَىٰ أَن يُعْرَفْنَ فَلَا يُؤْذَيْنَ وَكَانَ اللَّهُ غَفُورًا رَّحِيمًا (٥٩)"

الحجاب قبل الحساب. أَلْهَتْك الدنيا عن أمور دينك؟ لن تذوقي لذة حلاوة هذه الحياة إلا في طاعة الله.

ما وجهة نظرك عن الحجاب؟

Hijab

Dear reader, in our time, you cannot differentiate between a Muslim girl and a Christian girl!!!

Imagine with me where we have reached this point. By God, the heart will cry before the eyes. O Muslim woman, would you waste your hijab for a mortal world? God Almighty commanded us to wear the hijab to protect us from the scourges of the tongue of others, to protect us from the sick of the heart, because we are not like any other person. We are Muslim girls. No one can reach us that easily. Therefore, God has set controls for us regarding the hijab and mixing. We must wear the hijab as God Almighty commanded: that it be a covering. For all the body, and not to describe, and to be loose, so where are you from it? Do not listen to those who say that the hijab makes you older. You are a queen in the hijab.He said: "O Prophet, tell your wives and your daughters and the women of the believers to bring some of their cloaks over them. That is more likely that they should be recognized and not harmed. And God is Forgiving. " Merciful (59)"

Hijab before reckoning. Has the world distracted you from your religion? You will not taste the sweetness of this life except in obedience to God.

What is your view on the hijab?

أهمية الوقت

أبدا بهذا الحديث العظيم:-عن ابن عباس قال رسول الله صلى الله عليه وسلم "اغتنم خمسا قبل خمس: شبابك قبل هرمك، وصحتك قبل سقمك، وغناك قبل فقرك، وفراغك قبل شغلك، وحياتك قبل موتك" أخرجه الحاكم في المستدرك.

أهمية الوقت:-الوقت من أعظم النعم التي أنعمها الله علينا، فمن الواجب علينا أن نغتنمه ولا نهدره في أشياء لن تنفعنا، ولا ننس أننا سنسأل عليه أمام الله سبحانه وتعالى هناك أناس يتمنون الوقت الذي تلهوا فيه،و في الحديث السابق ذكره يقول رسولنا الكريم اغتنم خمسا قبل خمس وهي:-"شبابك قبل هرمك"، ذكر الشباب؛ لأنه الوقت الذي تكون فيه أكثر قوة وقادرا على التعلم واكتساب المهارات قبل أن يأت وقت الشيخوخة وتندم على هذا الوقت الذي لم تستفد منه بأي شيء، "صحتك قبل سقمك" كم من مريض يريد أن يتعافى أن يكون لديه صحة مثلك، أعمى يريد أن يبصر، وأصم يريد أن يسمع، وأبكم يريد أن يتكلم، وأنت مازلت لا تشكر الله على هذه النعمة، النعمة التي تعصي الله بها رغم أن هؤلاء الأشخاص يعبدون الله ويشكرونه على باقي النعم، وأنت تلهوا! "غناك قبل فقرك" أهؤلاء الفقراء ليس لهم من غناك شيء؟ أتشتري كل ما تشتهيه؟ وإخوانك يبكون؛ لأنهم جياع تخيل هذا! ستسأل أمام الله الله عنهم "فراغك قبل شغلك" اغتنم هذا الوقت في الطاعة والتعلم في مساعدتك لوالديك لا تقعد فارغا، فالفراغ كالسيف يقتل صاحبه "حياتك قبل مرضك" الحياة التي أعطاها الله لك؛ لتعبده وتفعل فيها كل ما يرضيه من عمل وعلم وغير ذلك هذه الحياة التي تذنب فيها فتتوب، ولا تشغلك هذه الحياة عن الله وتب دوما قبل أن يأتي الفارق الذي لا ينفع بعده توبة وهو الموت الكأس الذي سنشرب منه جميعا.

هل ستستمر في تضييع وقتك؟

The importance of time

Start with this great hadith: On the authority of Ibn Abbas, the Messenger of God, may God bless him and grant him peace, said, "Take advantage of five things before five things: your youth before your old age, your health before your sickness, your wealth before your poverty, your free time before your work, and your life before your death." Al-Hakim included it In Al-Mustadrak.

The importance of time: Time is one of the greatest blessings that God has bestowed upon us. It is our duty to seize It and not waste it on things that will not benefit us, and do not forget that we will be asked about it before God Almighty. There are people who wish for the time they had fun with, and in the aforementioned hadith, our noble Messenger says Take advantage of five things before five things, which are: - Your youth before your old age, remember youth; Because it is the time when you are stronger and able to learn and acquire skills before the time of old age comes and you regret this time that you did not benefit from anything,"Your health before your sickness" How many sick people want to recover and have health like you, a blind person who wants to see, a deaf person who wants to hear, and a mute person who wants to speak, and you still do not thank God for this blessing, the blessing with which you disobey God even though these people... They worship God and thank Him for the rest of the blessings, and you are having fun! "Your wealth comes before your poverty." Do these poor people have nothing from your wealth? Do you buy everything you want? And your brothers are crying; Because they are hungry imagine this! You will ask God about them before God, "Your free time comes before your busy time." Use this time to be obedient and learn to help your parents. Do not sit idle, for free time Is like a sword that kills its owner, "Your life before your illness" is the life that God gave you; To worship Him and do in it everything that pleases Him in terms of work, knowledge, and other things. This is the life in which you sin and repent. Do not let this life distract you from God and always repent before the difference comes after whichh repentance is of no use, which is death, the cup from which we will all drink.

Are you going to keep wasting your time?

التحدي

عندما كنت بالصف الثالث الثانوي قال لي شخص أنني سأظل فاشلا ، وعبثا على المجتمع ظلت كلماته تتردد في أذني لكنني لم أستسلم أبدا وتحديته أنني سأكون طبيبا ماهرا، وها قد مرت الأيام وصرت طبيبا كلمات ذاك الشخص مازادتني إلا تحدي وعزيمة ولم تؤثر عليّ بالسلب بل بفضله بعد الله عز وجل عرفت أنني على قدر كبير من المسؤولية، علينا جميعا أن نؤمن بقدراتنا، وأن كل الأحلام تتحقق، ولا تجعل كلمات الآخرين تؤثر عليك وعلى أحلامك، فأنت خلقت لتصنع مجدا، كن قويا وتحدى اليأس وليكن قدوتك الرسول صلى الله عليه وسلم عندما ذهب إلى الطائف ولم يؤمن به أحد لكنه لم ييأس وأكمل طريق دعوته، تحدي كل عقبة تقف أمامك، خلقت؛ لتجاهد لا لتستسلم وأجمل ما قيل في التحدي"أتتوعدنا بما ننتظر يا ابن اليهودية " تحدي الفشل... تحدي الإحباط... تحدي اليأس، أنت معجزة من الله تعالى.

The challenge

When I was in the third year of secondary school, a person told me that I would continue to be a failure, and that I would be a disservice to society. His words continued to echo in my ears, but I never gave up and challenged him that I would be a skilled doctor. Now, days have passed and I have become a doctor. That person's words only increased my challenge and determination, and they did not affect me negatively, but rather thanks to him. God Almighty, I knew that I had a great responsibility. We all have to believe in our abilities, and that all dreams come true, and do not let the words of others affect you and your dreams, for you were created to create glory, be strong and defy despair, Let your role model be the Messenger, may God bless him and grant him peace, when he went to Taif and no one believed in him, but he did not despair and continued on the path of his calling, challenging every obstacle that stands before you. You were created; To strive, not to surrender, and the most beautiful thing said in the challenge is: "Do you promise us what we are waiting for, son of Judaism?" The challenge of failure… the challenge of frustration… the challenge of despair. You are a miracle from God Almighty.

السوشيال ميديا

قارئي لنتعرف معا ما السوشيال ميديا؟

إنها سلاح ذو حدين إما أن تقضي عليه أو يُقضى عليك سأوضح أكثر لنأخذ السوشيال ميديا من الجانب الإيجابي:-لها إيجابيات كثيرة جدا من خلالها تستطيع أن تتواصل مع العالم الخارجي بأقصى سرعة، تستطيع أيضا أن تقم بعمل بحث بحضور محاضرات وغيرها من الأشياء التي تخص الدراسة، تستطيع أيضا أن تتعرف على أخبار من حولك وأن تكون أصدقاء جدد.... إلخ، الجانب السلبي:-تضيع كثيرا من وقتك عليها، تصبح أكثر إدمانا لها، تكون سبب في مشكلة كبيرة جدا لدى الأطفال الذين يُعطون الهاتف بكثرة وهي التوحد، وقد يتعرض حسابك للاختراق ويتم سرقة كل الصور وغيرها من الأشياء المهمة.... إلخ هذا يجعلنا أكثر حذرا منها على الرغم من مميزاتها، فا أنت تستطيع أن تحد من استخدامك لها، وذلك بطرق عدة منها تنظيم وقتك تجعل وقتا محددا تستخدم فيه السوشيال ميديا، وتذكر دوما أنك الحاكم لها وليس المحكوم منها، واعلم أن كل ما يقال على السوشيال ميديا ليس حقيقيا فقد ترى شخصا سعيدا عليها، وهو في الحقيقة قلبه يتمزق من الألم، فكن حذرا يا أخي، فهناك أمورا في حياتك أكثر أهمية من هذا الهراء.

Social media

Reader, let's learn together what social media is?

It Is a double-edged sword. Either you eliminate it or you are eliminated. I will explain more. Let's take social media from the positive side: It has many positives through whichh you can communicate with the outside world at maximum speed. You can also do research by attending lectures and other things related to study. You can also learn about the news of those around you and make new friends... etc. The negative side: - You waste a lot of your time on it, you become more addicted to it, it is the cause of a very big problem among children who are given the phone a lot, which is autism, and it may You're account is hacked and all photos and other important things are stolen...etc. This makes us more wary of it despite its advantages, so you can limit your use of it, This is done In several ways, including organizing your time, setting a specific time in whichh you use social media, and always remember that you are the ruler of it and not the ruled by it, and know that everything that is said on social media is not true. You may see a person happy on it, and in reality his heart is torn from pain, so be careful, my friend. Brother, there are more important things in your life than this nonsense.

العلاقات المحرمة

الله تعالى وضع لنا ضوابط الاختلاط؛ لكي يحمينا من مريضين القلب قال تعالى "يا نساء النبي لستن كأحد من النساء إن اتقيتن فلا تخضعن بالقول فيطمع الذي في قلبه مرض وقلن قولا معروفا" فا الله عز وجل لم ينهانا عن شيء قط إلا وفيه منفعة لنا فالاختلاط يطرأ عليه مفاسد كثيرة، فالاختلاط لا يكون إلا لضرورة فقط، وفي هذا الزمان ترى الفتيات والشباب يتكلمون مع بعضهم بحجة التعليم وغيرها من الأسباب التي لا تقبل، ومن جهة أخرى تراهم يقيمون علاقات غير شرعية بحجة أنهم يحبون بعضهم، وهذا كله عبث وإن حدث هذا وتزوجا فإن الله يكون غير راضي عن هذه العلاقة كم من بيوت خربت بسبب هذه العلاقات، فكل بداية لا ترضي الله عز وجل نهايتها لن ترضيك،قارئي العزيز أعلم أن الفتن انتشرت بكثرة لكن تذكر أن الله سيجازيك إن صبرت فاصبر واحتسب الأجر عند الله تعالى وسيرضيك، أما إن عصيته تعالى فانتظر وعيدك فعلى على الأيد ما كسبت إن خيرا فخير وإن شرا فشر، أترضى لأختك أن تتكلم مع شاب أجنبي عنها؟

بالطبع لن ترضى حتى وإن كان هذا الشاب يحبها بصدق لأنك تعلم يقينا عقلية هذا الشاب،هل ستستمر في هذه العلاقات المحرمة؟

Forbidden relationships

God Almighty has set the rules for mixing for us. In order to protect us from those who are sick at heart, God Almighty said, "O wives of the Prophet, you are not like any of the other women. If you fear God, do not be submissive in speech, lest he in whose heart is sickness become greedy, and speak words of kindness." God Almighty has never forbidden us from anything except that it is beneficial for us. Mixing brings about many evils, so mixing does not It is only out of necessity, and in this era you see girls and young men talking to each other under the pretext of education and other unacceptable reasons, and on the other hand you see them establishing illegal relationships under the pretext that they love each other, and this is all absurd, and if this happens and they get married, then God will be dissatisfied with this. Relationship: How many homes have been ruined because of these relationships. For every beginning that does not satisfy God Almighty, its end will not satisfy you, My dear reader, I know that temptations have spread widely, but remember that God will reward you if you are patient, so be patient and expect the reward from God Almighty and He will please you. But if you disobey Him, the Almighty, then wait for your threat. Then what you have earned is up to you. If it is good, then good, and If evil, then evil. Would you be satisfied with your sister speaking to a young man who is a stranger to her?

Of course, she will not be satisfied even if this young man truly loves her, because you know for sure the mentality of this young man. Will she continue In these forbidden relationships?

الخيانة

أيوجد أبشع من الخيانة؟

بلى، القلب الذي يخان يصبح فارغا، فاعتني بنفسك جيدا ولا تتركها كما فعل الآخرون، الخائنون لا أمان لهم وإن عادوا لنا من جديد أقلبك الجميل يستحق الخيانة؟ الأشخاص الخائنين يشبهون الظلام لن يضيؤوا أبدا مادامت قلوبهم تحمل السواد، الخيانة لا تأتي إلا من الأشخاص الذين منحناهم قلبنا بكل صدق لكنهم أعطونا درس لن ننساه، لا يوجد أمان لأي شخص، فأمانك ومأمنك الله الله فقط.

أومثل قلبي يخان؟

Treason

Is there anything worse than betrayal?

Yes, the heart that betrays becomes empty, so take good care of yourself and do not leave it like others did. Traitors have no security, even if they come back to us again, does your beautiful heart deserve betrayal? Disloyal people are like darkness. They will never light up as long as their hearts carry black. Betrayal only comes from people to whom we gave our heart in all sincerity, but they gave us a lesson that we will never forget. There is no safety for anyone, so your safety and security is God, God only.

Or is it like my heart being betrayed?

الأمانة

قارئي الأمانة هي أن تعطي لكل ذي حق حقه دون أن ينقص منه شيئا، ولا سيما إذا كان مسلما أو ذميا، فرسولنا الكريم عُرف بالصادق الأمين،" كان كل من يمتلك مالا أو شيئا يخاف عليه من السرقة يجعله عند رسول الله صلى الله عليه وسلم، وعندما اشتد أذى المشركين له أذن الله عز وجل له بالهجرة إلى المدينة،لكنه صلى الله عليه وسلم أمر سيدنا علي بن أبي طالب رضي الله عنه وأرضاه أن يرد تلك الأمانات إلى أهلها وكان عنده أمانات كثيرة لهؤلاء الكفار وغيرهم، هذا رسولنا الكريم رغم كل ما فعلوه الكفار معه كان أمينا، فهذا واجب علينا فأُمرنا من الله تعالى أن نؤدي الأمانات إلى أهلها، فالشخص الأمين يحب الله ورسوله؛ لامتثاله لطاعتهم ، ماذا لو كان المجتمع كله أمينا، بالطبع سيعم الخير، وتنتشر المحبة بين أفراده، فلم أر شخصا أمينا إلا أحبه الناس، فالأمانة صفة يجب أن يمتلكها أي شخص كان، وأجمل ما قيل في تحميل الأمانات!

"بلغوا سلامنا لرسول الله صلى الله عليه وسلم"

Honesty

The meaning of trust is to give every rightful person his due without subtracting anything from him, especially if he is a Muslim or a non-Muslim. Our noble Messenger was known as the honest and trustworthy. "Everyone who owned money or something for fear of being stolen would keep it with the Messenger of God, may God bless him and grant him peace. When the polytheists harmed him intensified, God Almighty permitted him to migrate to Medina, but he, may God's prayers and peace be upon him, ordered our master Ali bin Abi Talib, may God be pleased with him, to return those trusts to their owners, and he had many trusts for these infidels and others. This is our noble Messenger, despite everything they did. The unbelievers with him were trustworthy, so this is our duty, so we were commanded by God Almighty to return the trusts to their owners, An honest person loves God and His Messenger. For his compliance with their obedience. What if the entire society were honest? Of course goodness would prevail, and love would spread among its members. I have never seen an honest person except that people loved him. Honesty is a quality that any person must possess, and the most beautiful thing that has been said about the burden of trustworthiness!

"Convey our greetings to the Messenger of God, may God bless him and grant him peace."

الظلم

قارئي ما هو الظلم؟

أرى الظلم وكأنه نقطة حبر سقطت في كأس به ماء، علينا أن نقض على هذا الفعل الشنيع، ونبتعد عنه، فلن يتقدم مجتمع يسود الظلم فيه، فالعدل أساس التقدم والرقي، نحن الآن نعيش في عصر تكاثر فيه الظلم وأصبح شيئا معتادا، وكأنهم نسوا أن الله سبحانه وتعالى حرم الظلم على نفسه وجعله بيننا محرما، لا تحزن أيها المظلوم، فلك الديان الذي لا يضيع حقك.

أما والله إن الظلم شؤم

ولا زال المسيء هو المظلوم

إلى الديان يوم الدين نمضي

وعند الله تجتمع الخصوم

عجبا لك يا ابن آدم تظلم ولا تحب أن تُظْلم! أيوجد أقبح من الظلم في هذه الحياة؟

Injustice

Reader: What is Injustice?

I see injustice as a drop of Ink that fell into a cup of water. We must eradicate this heinous act and stay away from it. A society in which injustice prevails will not advance. Justice is the basis of progress and progress. We now live in an era in which injustice has multiplied and has become a common thing. It is as if they have forgotten that God Glory be to Him, the Almighty, has forbidden injustice for Himself and made it forbidden among us. Do not be sad, O oppressed person, for you are the judge who does not waste your rights.

By God, injustice is bad news

The abuser Is still the oppressed

To the Judge on the Day of Judgment we go

With God, adversaries meet

It is amazing that you, son of Adam, do injustice and do not like to be wronged! Is there anything worse than injustice in this life?

الحلم

تحديد الهدف والاستمرار على تحقيقه، وأن نثق بالله تعالى ثم بأنفسنا أننا قادرين على تحقيقه يعطينا طاقة إيجابية، مهما مررت بالصعاب في سبيل تحقيقك لحلمك لا تستسلم أبدا، فأقوى المعارك يعطيها الله لأقوى جنوده، ومهما كثروا الأشخاص السلبيين حولك، فكن لنفسك الشخص الإيجابي ولا يهمك ما يقال عنك، فأنت الوحيد من يعرف نفسه جيدا، كلنا معجزات من الله سبحانه وتعالى خلقنا مميزين، فلا تجعل كلام الناس يؤثر فيك، واستعن بالله تعالى وسيأتيك التوفيق أينما حلت خطاك،واعلم أن حياتك لن تتكرر مرتين، فا اجعل كل لحظة تعيشها وكأنها آخر لحظة، واستغل كل ثانية فيها، كي لا تندم بعد فوات الأوان.

قارئي أما حان أن نترك منطقة الراحة وننطلق إلى الأمام؟

The dream

Setting a goal and continuing to achieve it, and trusting in God Almighty and then ourselves that we are able to achieve it gives us positive energy. No matter how many difficulties you go through in order to achieve your dream, never give up. The strongest battles God gives to his strongest soldiers, and no matter how many negative people are around you, be the positive person for yourself and do not care. What is said about you, you are the only one who knows himself well. We are all miracles from God Almighty. He created us special. Do not let people's words affect you. Seek help from God Almighty and success will come to you wherever you take your step. Know that your life will not be repeated twice, so make every moment you live as if it were your last. Moment, and take advantage of every second, so that you do not regret it when it is too late.

Reader, is it not time for us to leave the comfort zone and move forward?

الوفاء

نحن الآن نعيش في عصر يُطعن المرء فيه من أحب الأشخاص إليه بسيف المين، نرى أصدقاؤنا يمدحوننا أمام أعيننا ولكن خلف ظهورنا يقال فينا أبغض الأشياء تُرى ما السبب؟

إنه فقدان الوفاء الذي يجعل مجتمعنا مترابط ومحب، وقد حثنا الإسلام على الوفاء بالعهود والمواثيق مما يدل على سمة هذه الصفة، الأوفياء كالقمر ساطعين دوما، الإنسان الوفي يكون محبا لأصدقائه ووالديه ومخلصا لهم، يكن بالشكر لمن لهم عليه حق، فهو إنسان لا ينس من عانوا لأجله، والناس يحبون من يتودد لهم، الوفاء يجعلنا نحب بعضنا،أيها القارئ كن وفيا وإن تعرضت للخذلان، فا الله لن يضيع كل هذا عبثا فالخير ينتصر دوما وإن قل.

"مات الوفاء فلا رفد ولا طمع

في الناس لم يبق إلا اليأس والجذع"

Fulfillment

We now live in an era in whichh the most beloved people are stabbed with a sword. We see our friends praising us in front of our eyes, but behind our backs the most hateful things are said about us. What is the reason?

It Is the loss of loyalty that makes our society interconnected and loving. Islam has urged us to fulfill covenants and covenants, which indicates the characteristic of this trait. Loyal people are like the moon, always shining. A loyal person is loving and loyal to his friends and parents. He is grateful to those who have rights over him. He is a person who does not forget those who have suffered. For his sake, people love those who court them. Loyalty makes us love each other. O reader, be loyal even if you are betrayed. God will not waste all of this In vain, for goodness always triumphs, even if It is small.

"Loyalty is dead, so there is neither greed nor greed

There is nothing left in the people except despair and despair."

الصدق

لم أر في حياتي شيئا أعظم الصدق، كونك صادقا هذا يرفع من قيمتك عند الله تعالى وعند رسوله صلى الله عليه وسلم حيث قال صلى الله عليه وسلم "عليكم بالصدق، فإن الصدق يهدي إلى البر وإن البر يهدي إلى الجنة، وما يزال الرجل يصدق ويتحري الصدق حتى يكتب عند الله صديقا..." والصدق يكون في أشياء كثيرة، لكن أعظمه أن تكون صادقا مع الله تعالى، ولا شك أن الشخص الذي يصدق مع الله يصدق معه كل شيء ، فلابد من الصدق في القول والعمل حتى في المزح يجب أن تكون صادقا هذا يدل على قيمة الصدق العظيمة، وأن الكذب ريبة، والناس يبغضون الكذب فعليك التحلي بالصدق كي تنال رضا الله عز وجل ومحبة رسوله صلى الله عليه وسلم

عليك بالصدق يا مخلوق يا أنسان

بالصدق تكسب رضى الباري وغفرانه

الصدق منجاة لأربابه من النيران

والله صادق بحدذاته وسبحانه

لا ترضي الناس فيما يغضب الرحمن

من سار بالصدق ما يُمناآ بخُسرانه

علينا أن نعي أهمية الصدق في حياتنا، وأنه لو فُقد كنا جميعا لاشيء، وليكن شعارك في هذه الحياة الصدق فبه نتقدم، وقد وصف حبيبنا صلى الله عليه وسلم ب "الصادق الأمين" أليس علينا أن نتشبه برسولنا صلى الله عليه وسلم؟

Honesty

I have never seen anything greater in my life than honesty. Being honest raises your value before God and you are His Messenger, may God's prayers and peace be upon him. He, may God's prayers and peace be upon him, said, "You must be honest, for honesty leads to righteousness and righteousness leads to heaven, and a person still believes and deserves honesty." Until he is recorded with God as a friend…" Honesty is in many things, but the greatest of them is to be honest with God, and there is no doubt that the person who is honest with God Is honest with him in everything, so he must be honest in the legal statement, even in jest, he must be honest. This indicates the value of complete honesty, and that lying is suspicious, and people hate lying. Be honest in order to gain the satisfaction of God Almighty and the love of His Messenger, may God bless him and grant him peace, You must be honest, O human being

By being honest, you gain the Creator's approval and forgiveness

Honesty saves its masters from hellfire

God is truthful in Himself and Glory be to Him

Do not please people while the Most Gracious is angry

Whoever follows the truth will never lose it

We have to be aware of the importance of honesty in our lives, and that if it were lost, we would all be nothing, and let your motto In this life be honesty, for with it we advance. Our Beloved, may God bless him and grant him peace, was described as "truthful and trustworthy." Shouldn't we imitate our Messenger, may God bless him and grant him peace?

الكذب

أيستحق أحد أن تكذب لأجله؟

بلى، نرى شخصا يمزح كذبا، يكذب على والديه، يكذب على صديقه، وهذا كله بحجة أنها كذبة بيضاء، قارئي لا يوجد في الإسلام كذب أبيض وكذب أسود بل هو كذب، ولم يبح الإسلام الكذب إلا في ثلاث"الإصلاح بين الناس، والحرب، وحديث الرجل امرأته والمرأة زوجها"فمن كذب في غيرهم عوقب، والكذب أقصر طريق إلى النار كما قال الرسول صلى الله عليه وسلم "الكذب يهدي إلى الفجور، وإن الفجور يهدي إلى النار وما يزال العبد يكذب ويتحى الكذب حتى يكتب عند الله كذابا" فالمؤمن لا يكذب أبدا، وتذكر قوله تعالى "ومن أظلم ممن افترى على الله كذبا"كن صادقا حتى وإن كان الصدق يعود عليك بالضرر يكفي أنك امتثلت لقوله تعالى" يا أيها الذين ءامنوا اتقوا الله وكونوا مع الصادقين "

ابتعد دوما عن الأشخاص الكذابين حتى لا تصاب بمرض الكذب، فا إنه المرض الأخطر على الإطلاق، وعلاجه صعب جدا.

Lying

Does anyone deserve to lie for them?

Yes, we see someone joking, lying to his parents, lying to his friend, and all of this under the pretext that it is a white lie. My reader, there is no white lie and a black lie in Islam. Rather, it is a lie. Islam does not permit lying except in three cases: reconciliation between people, war, and hadith. A man is his wife and a woman is her husband. So whoever lies about others will be punished, and lying is the shortest path to Hell, as the Messenger, may God bless him and grant him peace, said, "Lying leads to immorality, and immorality leads to Hell. The servant will continue to lie and avoid lying until he is recorded with God as a liar."The believer never lies, and remember the Almighty's saying, "And who is more unjust than he who invents a lie against God?" Be honest, even if the truth will cause you harm. It is sufficient that you complied with the Almighty's saying, "O you who have believed, fear God and be with the truthful."

Always stay away from lying people so that you do not contract the disease of lying, as it is the most dangerous disease of all, and its treatment is very difficult.

العمل

قارئي العزيز العمل أساس ورقعة كل المجتمعات، فبدونه لا قيمة للحياة، فالله سبحانه وتعالى أمرنا أن نعمل ونجتهد؛ لكي ننال رضاه ثم مبتغانا، ولقد جعلنا الله خلائف في الأرض؛ لنعمرها بالعمل الذي يرضيه، وقد كرمنا سبحانه وتعالى على كثير ممن خلق، وجعلنا مميزين بعقولنا، فالرجل يعمل ليطعم صغاره، والشاب يعمل ليحقق رغباته بجني المال، لنلق نظرة على الدول المتقدمة سنجد وقت العمل أكثر من وقت الراحة نعم هذه الدول المتقدمة، فا أين نحن من هذا؟ ولا تنس قوله تعالى "وقل اعملوا فسيرى الله عملكم ورسوله"

هل سألت نفسك يوما ما هو عملك؟ وهل يرضي الله تعالى ورسوله؟

The job

Dear reader, work is the foundation and foundation of all societies. Without it, life has no value. God Almighty has commanded us to work and strive. In order to obtain His satisfaction and our desire, God has made us successors on earth. Let us populate it with work that pleases Him. God Almighty has honored many of those He has created, and made us distinguished by our minds. The man works to feed his children, and the young man works to fulfill his desires by earning money. Let us take a look at the developed countries. We will find more time for work than time for rest. Yes, these are developed countries, so where are we? Who is this? And do not forget the Almighty's saying, "And say, 'Work, for God and His Messenger will see your work.'"

Have you ever asked yourself what your job is? Does God Almighty and His Messenger please?

الصبر

الصبر من أعظم العبادات، وأشقها على الإنسان لذا جعل الله ثوابه كبير، فكلنا بلا استثناء يوجد في حياتنا غصة تعكر صفونا، ولكن الصبر والتحمل والرضا بها سيرفعنا درجات في الجنان، أعلم أنه من الصعب أن نتحمل، ولكن هذه الحياة وهذا القضاء والقدر ولا يؤمن أحدنا إلا بإيمانه بالقضاء والقدر، ولا تجعل همومك تنسيك الغاية التي خُلقت لأجلها وهي عبادة الله عز وجل، وتيقن أن الله سيجزيك على صبرك وتحملك،،فربك رحيم ودود كن راضيا بما قسمه الله لك، وسيرضيك عز وجل ويجبر كسرك وحزنك، ولا تتأفف وتسخط فربك أيضا العزيز الجبار، وليكن همك الأكبر هو إرضاء الله تعالى، وإن كنت في بحر يموج فيه الآلام، وكن مطمئنا بأن لك رب لن يضيعك أبدا، بالله عليك انظر إلى إخواننا في فلسطين انظر إلى صبرهم، وقوة إيمانهم، وحسن ظنهم بالله يحدث أن أحدهم يفقد أولاده، ثم يقول" المهم ترضى يارب" أي صبر هذا؟

تذكر معي كم صبر الرسول صلى الله عليه وسلم على أذى المشركين ولم ييأس أبدا، وأنت مجرد أن قابتلك مشكلة تأففت وسببت العيش!

تذكر دوما كلما تقابلك عقبة قوله عز وجل "الذين إذا أصابتهم مصيبة قالوا إنا لله وإنا إليه راجعون أولئك عليهم صلوات من ربهم ورحمة وأولئك هم المهتدون"

تذكر أيضا قول سيدنا علي رضي الله عنه وأرضاه سأصبر حتى يعجز الصبر عن صبري

سأصبر حتى ينظر الرحمن في أمري

سأصبر حتى يعلم الصبر

أني صبرت على شيء أمر من الصبر

ألا تستحق الجنة منك أن تصبر على هذه المشقات؟

Patience

Patience is one of the greatest acts of worship, and the most difficult for a person, so God made its reward great. We all, without exception, have a problem in our lives that disturbs our peace, but patience, endurance, and being satisfied with It will raise us degrees in heaven. I know that it is difficult to bear, but this life and this decree and destiny and none of us believe. Except by his belief in destiny and destiny, and do not let your worries make you forget the purpose for which you were created, which is the worship of God Almighty, and be certain that God will reward you for your patience and endurance, for your Lord is merciful and friendly. Be content with what God has divided for you, and the Almighty will satisfy you and heal your brokenness and sadness, and do not be discouraged and angry, for your Lord also Dear Mighty,Let your greatest concern be to please God Almighty, even if you are in a sea full of pain, and be reassured that you have a God who will never waste you. For God's sake, look at our brothers in Palestine, look at their patience, the strength of their faith, and their good faith in God. It happens that one of them loses his children, then he says "The important thing is that you are satisfied, O Lord." What kind of patience is this?Remember with me how patient the Messenger, may God bless him and grant him peace, was in the face of the harm of the polytheists and never gave up, even though you were faced with a problem that troubled you and caused you to live!

Always remember whenever you encounter an obstacle, the Almighty said: "Those who, when a calamity befalls them, say, 'Indeed, to Allah we belong, and to Him we shall return.' Those are upon them blessings from their Lord and mercy, and those are the ones who are guided."

Remember also the saying of our master Ali, may God be pleased with him and please him: I will be patient until my patience is no longer possible

I will be patient until the Most Merciful looks into my matter

I will be patient until he learns patience

I was patient with something very patient

Doesn't Heaven deserve you to be patient with these hardships ؟

عادات يومية

قل لي أين أنت من صلاتك؟ أين وردك وأذكارك؟ أين أنت من قيام الليل؟

ولتكن صلاتك ووردك وأذكارك الجزء الأكثر أهمية في حياتك، فوالله من حافظ عليهن فتح الله عليه أبواب الرزق والنجاح والتوفيق، لا تقل لي لا يوجد وقت فا ساعة واحدة لن تنقص من وقتك بل ستبارك في وقتك وتجعلك تحقق أشياء كثير ترغب في فعلها، لماذا لم تحافظ على قيام الليل؟

ألم ترد أن تتحقق أمانيك؟

قيام الليل يحقق المعجزات، فالله تبارك وتعالى ينزل إلى السماء الدنيا اطلب منه كل ما تريد، فا أنت تطلب من رب المستحيل الذي إن قال للشيء كن فيكون بالطبع سيكون سبحانه وتعالى قادر مقتدر على تحقيق أمانيك، وستكون نصيحتي الأبدية لك أيها القارئ أن تحافظ عليهن وسترى العجب العجاب في حياتك.

Daily habits

Tell me where you are in your prayers? Where are your roses and remembrances? Where are you during the night prayer?

Let your prayers, supplications, and remembrances be the most important part of your life. By God, whoever maintains them, God will open the doors of sustenance, success, and success to him. Do not tell me that there is no time, for one hour will not detract from your time, but rather it will bless your time and make you achieve many things that you desire to do. Why did you not preserve it? On the night prayer?

Didn't you want your wishes to come true?

Praying at night achieves miracles. God, Blessed and Most High, descends to the lowest heaven. Ask Him for everything you want. You are asking the Lord of the impossible, who if He said to something, "Be," and it will be. Of course, God Almighty will be able and powerful to fulfill your wishes. My eternal advice to you, the reader, will be to preserve them and you will see. Wonder is the wonder in your life.

الوحدة

أسير وحدي في طريق مظلم التفت في كل مكان لا أجد أحد يساندني أكمل سيري فإذا بي أرى صديقين حميمين يضحكان ويتشاكلان مع بعضهما تمنيت أن لو كان لي صديقا، أكملت سيري فإذا بحبيبين يعطي أحدهما للآخر وردة ويقول سامحني سرت وأنا شاردة لا أستطيع التكلم فقط أبكي فإذا بشاحنة تكاد أن تدعسني لكن كان هناك من انتشلني من أمامها بسرعة، فعرفت أن الله بعثه؛ لأعرف أني لم أكن وحيدة وأن الله تعالى معي يا رفاق ربما لا نكون جميعا لدينا صديق أو حبيب لكن لا تنس ولو للحظة أن الله معك.

تُرى ما أجمل الوحدة التي تكون فيها مع الله؟

Unit

I'm walking alone on a dark road. I turn around everywhere, and I can't find anyone to support me. I continue my walk, and then I see two good friends laughing and arguing with each other. I wished I had a friend. I continue my walk, and then two lovers give each other a rose and say, "Forgive me. I walked while I was distracted. I can't speak. I just cry." A truck almost ran me over, but someone quickly pulled me out of it, so I knew that God had sent him. To know that I was not alone and that God Almighty is with me. Guys, we may not all have a friend or lover, but do not forget, even for a moment, that God Is with you.

Do you think how beautiful is the unity in which you are with God?

الخذلان

قارئي العزيز هل تعرف ماهو الخذلان؟

الخذلان صفعة قوية تأخذها ممن كنت تظن بهم خيرا ممن كنت تحبهم لم أر في حياتي شعور أصعب من الخذلان، أتساءل لماذا يأتي من أناس أحببناهم بصدق؟ الخذلان من أصعب المواقف التي تمر علينا حيث لا نستطيع أن ننس من خذلنا بهذه السهولة، فلربما كان صديق أو حبيب أو قريب، أرى الخذلان كأخ يسفك دم أخيه كشخص يحمل السواد في قلبه! لا بأس علينا أن نحيا من جديد وتشرق ابتسامتنا، علينا جميعا أن نعلم أننا لا نستحق إلا المحبة ممن حولنا وأننا خلقنا لنحب بعضنا ونتعاون؛ لتعمير هذه الأرض، ولا نفسدها بكرهنا لبعضنا البعض.

Let down

Dear reader, do you know what betrayal is?

Letdown is a strong slap, take it from those whom you thought were better than those whom you loved. I have never seen anything more beautiful than disappointment in my life. I wonder why It comes from people we truly loved? Letdown is one of the most beautiful forests we inflict on us, as it is of no use to forget the one who let us down so easily, perhaps it was a friend, lover, or relative, who sees letdown as someone who sheds his brother's blood as a person with blackness in his heart! It is okay for us to live again and let our smile shine. We must all know that we only deserve to have loved ones around us and that we were created to love each other and cooperate. To rebuild this land, and not spoil it by hating each other.

الحنين

أشتاق للحظات كانت تجمعنا، أرى كل الوجوه كأنها أنت رحلت عني وتركتني وحدي أسيرة الذكريات المؤلمة أتخيل لو كنت معي كيف ستبدو الحياة؟ بالطبع ستكون أكثر من رائعة، وسنعيش أنا وأنت في كوكب آخر مليء بالفرح والطمأنينة أشتاق إليك يا أبي في كل لحظة تمر علي سيبقى قلبي يحبك دوما، وستبقى أجمل الرجال في نظري، حب الأب لا مثيل له مهما كبر المرء منا يحتاج إلى والده الآباء بالنسبة لنا كالأكسجين لا نستطع أن نستغني عنهم.

Nostalgia

I miss the moments that brought us together. I see all the faces as if you left me alone, a prisoner of painful memories. I imagine if you were with me, what would life be like? Of course, it will be more than wonderful, and you and I will live on another planet full of joy and tranquility. I miss you, father, in every moment that passes by. My heart will always love you, and you will remain the most beautiful of men in my eyes. A father's love is unparalleled, no matter how old one of us gets. He needs his father. Fathers for us. Like oxygen, we cannot do without them.

التدخين

إن التدخين في زماننا هذا يمثل الكارثة الكبرى حيث انتشر بكثرة في القرون الأخيرة، مسلمون ونصارى وغيرهم ممن يشربون المسكر أستغرب كثيرا لماذا الإنسان يشتري السجائر أو أشياء من هذا الصنف ويعلم أنها تضره؟

قارئي كل هذا يضرك ويسلب منك صحتك لم تمتنع عنه؟ فلقد أثبتت دراسات أن السيجارة الواحدة تقضي على الآلاف من خلايا الرأس، وتسبب سرطان الرئة وضيق التنفس وتؤدي إلى الوفاة ما الذي يجبرك على شراء هذه السموم؟ فوالله لا يستحق شيء أن تدمر نفسك بسببه، كثير من الناس يقولون بأنها تعطي لهم بعضا من الراحة وهذا كله عبث، لكي تشعر بالراحة هناك قرآن هناك صلاة ادعوا الله أن يشفي عليل فؤادك وتذكر قوله تعالى "وإذا سألك عبادي عني فإني قريب أجيب دعوة الداعي" سل الله أن يبعدك عن هذا البلاء، معاشر الشباب اتقوا الله في أموالكم وأنفسكم، واقطع وعدا من هذا اليوم أنك لن تشرب هذه المحرمات وأنك أقوى من أن تحطمك سيجارة.

Smoking

Smoking in our time represents the greatest disaster, as it has spread widely in recent centuries. Muslims, Christians, and others who drink intoxicants. I am surprised why a person buys cigarettes or things of this type and knows that they harm him?

Reader, all this harms you and takes away your health. Why didn't you abstain from it? Studies have proven that one cigarette destroys thousands of brain cells, causes lung cancer, shortness of breath, and leads to death. What forces you to buy these toxins? By God, nothing is worth destroying yourself because of it. Many people say that it gives them some comfort, and this is all in vain. In order for you to feel comfortable, there is the Qur'an, there is prayer. Pray to God to heal the sickness of your heart, and remember the Almighty's saying, "And when My servants ask you about Me, then I am near, and I answer the call of the supplicant." Ask God to keep you away from this calamity, Young people, fear God with your money and your souls, and make a promise from this day that you will not drink these forbidden things and that you are stronger than a cigarette to destroy you.

الفـهرس